HOW TO FIND YOURSELF, LOVE YOURSELF, & BE YOURSELF:
The Secret Instruction Manual for Being Human

by

STEPHEN LOVEGROVE

ISBN-13: 978-1507764039
ISBN-10: 1507764030

For Melissa, Micah, and Bryce

Because all of you deserve a life you love

Table of Contents

Introduction

I remember the autumn night as clearly as I do the Gossip Girl Finale and the Beyonce halftime show, and that's saying a lot. But unlike that CW drama and that performance from a pop icon, this night is not a fond memory. Rather, this moment which I can still vividly recall was one of the most difficult moments of self-reflection which I have experienced.

I stared at myself in the strange hazy lighting of my bathroom mirror. I couldn't stop crying. This fact in and of itself alarmed me, because for so long, I hadn't been able to cry. And now, here I was, weeping.

It didn't feel therapeutic. I know scientists promise that all the negative hormones are being released as you cry, but I didn't notice my emotional stability rising as the tears fell. I just knew I was crying, and my whole body was shaking, and I couldn't make it stop.

When I looked in the mirror, I saw eyes that carried so much more sorrow than they knew how to hide. I saw a face full of wrinkles that were the result of stress and anxiety far beyond what should have been my experience at that age. I knew that I was breathing, which meant life had to keep going. But I honestly had no desire for it to continue at that point. I couldn't come up with even one semi-plausible reason why waking up tomorrow would be a good thing, and I couldn't find a single piece of evidence that indicated things would get better.

What was the problem, you ask? What was hurting me so badly that night? I wouldn't have been able to put it in words if you asked me then. I knew that it wasn't a specific person or incident or situation. Nothing external had triggered this breakdown. I just knew something was not right. My life was not working, and I was not okay with that. The wisdom of hindsight would reveal that I had no clue how to find myself, no idea how to love myself, and no ability to be myself. Mix all of those three dilemmas, and you've created a cocktail that will knock anyone out.

Even though I couldn't name those specific issues that night, I did own where I was to the best of my ability. That's often all we can do in a crisis. So that night, I looked myself in the eyes and said, "It isn't supposed to be this way."

Five years later, on another autumn night, just as dark and just as chilly outside, I found myself in a very different place internally.

I had been invited to attend Oprah's first national tour. This event felt significant, as everyone knew it was the first time she had ever done an arena live show, and it might be the last. I can still remember exactly where my seat was in that arena. The press section was full of enthusiastic and motivated individuals, happy to hand out business cards and talk about their ideas. I got to experience the entire tour sitting next to a blogger from my network, a friend who knew all the right questions to ask that weekend to make sure I was able to process everything.

And I will never forget one transformative moment from the end of that experience. Oprah was just about to say goodbye, to thank us for coming to her tour and to wish us all the best in pursuing the life we wanted. But right before she went off stage, she read us a poem - a poem which I will share with you later in this book.

As she read, I instinctively gave myself a hug. It was a habit I had picked up from zumba class a couple summers before, one that I hadn't used often since then. But I knew that moment called for a hug.

I embraced myself, feeling the warmth of my body heat and the pulse of my heartbeat. On an enormous backdrop behind the stage, the sun went down and stars filled the LED display. Twinkling lights appeared all around the Verizon Center. And I suddenly felt tears in my eyes.

It was startling. Those tears were the first ones which had greeted me in a while, and they caught me off guard. This felt like another mirror moment for me. Only this time, I wasn't looking in as an outsider. This time, I saw myself through myself, from within myself. And the tears that accompanied this reflective gaze were completely different.

I knew who I was now. I had figured out how to love myself. And more and more each day, I was learning to be myself in the world. Life felt completely different, like I was sipping the perfection of a made-to-order drink that was exactly what I had imagined. As I looked up at the stars right then, I found myself saying, "This is what it was supposed to be like all along."

Do you see yourself in either of those mirror moments? I'd be overjoyed to hear that you identified with the last one. Whenever someone tells me that they are loving life in every possible way, my heart soars and shares in their joy.

But sadly, I know that experience is not the reality of many people's lives right now. In one way or another, it's far more likely you can relate to that first mirror moment - the one that happened in the tiny bathroom with the khaki walls and the Finding Nemo bathtub stickers.

Are you unsatisfied with your life? If so, can you begin here by admitting that out loud? I know exactly what that feels like and just how much it sucks. It's easy to think that if we had a different house, different car, different job, different relationship, different city, everything would be different; that we would *feel* different then.

The problem is, you are the main character in the story that is your life. No matter how much you alter the setting of that story, you can't escape from yourself. There are many factors which contribute to your experience on this planet, but ultimately, you are the one creating your experience here. In order to get to the life you are here to live, you must begin by becoming the person you are here to become. There is no way around it.

How do you get there? The solution is simple while simultaneously extensive.

You do the work to find yourself, love yourself, and be yourself.

Yes, it's a ton of work, not always the easiest process either. But what I know for sure is that until you are willing to do this work, you will find it difficult, if not impossible, to love your life. You will get stuck approaching each day with dread, stress, frustration, and apathy.

And you don't have to! There is a different way to exist. It is indeed possible to love your life. And that's why you are reading this book. As I went through my intense five year journey of personal growth, I wished that there was an instruction manual for all of it. Surely there were people who had gone before me in this process. I knew there were people out there who had found themselves, loved themselves, and were able to be themselves, and I could use all the help I could get in starting over.

I ended up gathering that information from all over the place - personal experiences, conversations with people, books, podcasts, songs, films, random strangers in pubs, spiritual teachers, even the least spiritual television shows imaginable. And I tried to take everything I know and put it into this book for you, so that you will feel like you were finally given the secret instruction manual to teach you how to be a human being.

You are going to find yourself, love yourself, and be yourself. You are going to love your life. All of this is possible for you. But it doesn't happen overnight. And it doesn't just happen by reading words on a page. It happens when you decide to make an investment in yourself - to do the work of healing that is long overdue.

That's what we're going to do here. I'm going to walk you through the process step by step. In every chapter, I'll show you what this journey looked like for me. I'll give you powerful questions to ask yourself for personal reflection, and if you're really serious about seeing change NOW, every chapter will end with a practical tool you can practice today.

How do I know this works? I would never sell you anything or even give you anything if I doubted its credibility. But I stand by the words of this book, because I lived them. These pages are not filled with random musings that popped into my head one day. Instead, they give you an inside look at the journey I took to love my life. This book contains the very heart and soul of the life I live - the energy I operate from each day that makes my life as magical as it is.

If this process can work for me, I *promise* it can work for you. Remember - I didn't start out as a personal life coach speaking to, writing to, and working with individuals around the world. This journey began for me in that tiny bathroom with the undersized mirror. All I had was a conviction that life didn't have to be this way; the hope that if I was willing to do the work - I really could love my life.

And I found out that was indeed possible.

If I can start from a personal rock bottom and end up with a magical life, I know for sure that anyone can. Everybody has the capability to love their life.

As I've shared this message with an international audience, I've had countless people tell me that it's helped them discover who they were. I've heard story after story from people of how this message helped them love themselves for the first time in their entire life. People from all walks of life have taken the information you are about to encounter and blossomed inside & out because of it.

Simply put, this book works.

My invitation to you is simple:

Come with me. Read. Listen. Open your heart.

If I give you a question to ponder, answer it.

If I suggest an exercise that might be of assistance, give it a try.

If I prompt you to let your heart go places it hasn't in a while, take a risk and dive in.

What I can promise is that you will receive out of this book in proportion to the investment you make *in yourself* while reading it.

So decide now that you are worth it. Decide that you deserve to find yourself. To love yourself. To truly be yourself.

If you do, I promise you will set this book down when you finish it a different human being - more real and true and authentic to who you were always meant to be.

Now, there are always people at this point who get tempted to close the book and stop reading - to put it off and continue later, or to indefinitely table this process. And I understand how tempting that is. I know embarking on this path may sound scary or difficult or overwhelming. You have the option now, and at any point, to decide it isn't worth it. Your personal growth has to be your choice.

But I like to think of this as an ocean. Like a beautiful, majestic, and awe-inspiring sea awaits you. And you are welcome to enter however you see fit - to wade, to walk lightly, to swim for your life, or to sail. The decision is yours. No one will stop you from returning to the sandy towel on the shore if you desire.

But I'd like to think you chose to come to the sea for a reason. You have been called to the sea. There is something here that you need, and it has awaited your arrival for quite some time.

Don't turn back now. You don't want things to stay the same. Maybe right now, that doesn't sound so bad, sure. It seems actually quite convenient for the time being. But there is something inside you that declares that you actually desire more. That's why we're both here on this page.

Let's take a step in. Let's see what the ocean has in store. Aren't you at least a little curious to see what happens in your heart in chapter one? I sure am.

Happy sailing!

Stephen

Chapter One

At the beginning of every chapter, I will give you a short explanation of why that chapter is in the book. I made sure not to waste any of your time writing this book. But to help you know what value to be on the lookout for in each section, I begin with a humorously titled blurb, "Don't Skip This Chapter."

Don't Skip This Chapter...
because I share the one thing I ask from you as you read that I know will give you the best possible experience

"You've got to find yourself first. Everything else will follow."
~ Charles DeLint

One premise should be understood from the first page of this book. I wrote all of these words because I believe in <u>you.</u> To me, you are not ultimately a reader, a client, a customer, or a statistic.

You are a soul. You are a creator. You are an individual, absolutely and positively one of a kind. You are an energetic being of love with enough power inside of you to change this entire world forever. That is who you are, and I am sitting down to write all of this precisely because I believe that about you.

I think you are worth any investment. To be honest with you, I enjoy writing about as much as I do LA traffic. Even though I have to create content for various publications every week, it's never a task I look forward to. Public speaking? Exhilarating. Interviews? Mind blowing. Coaching people one-on-one? What I do best. But writing is not my passion. Embarrassingly enough, I knew I was supposed to write this book for a full three months before I put words down on a page. We all struggle to push ourselves into large personal investments, don't we? But once I finally sat down and started writing, a full sixty pages came out all at once. This book began to flow through me effortlessly, and I knew I was operating in a calling by writing to you.

I made myself push past the resistance and start writing because I knew this book would have the power to change you. I knew these words would be able to release something new and special and wonderful into your life. Because I believe you are worth the investment, I wrote to you.

So I believe in this book with all my heart. Every word, every idea, every page - it comes to you directly from me. I believe this book is about to unleash something new in your journey, open something new in your heart, and plant something new in your soul.

I only ask one thing in return. Would you read this with all of yourself? Please don't enter this book half-heartedly, expecting a couple interesting stories and a few recycled thoughts. Bring your whole self to this space.

My suggestion is that you always have a blank piece of paper next to you each time you begin a chapter. There are exercises and questions for you to work through, and paper will make those much easier. But you also need to have paper there just in case. You need to be ready if something talks on the inside of you, if something pops into your head, if something is felt deep within. Have that paper there at all times when reading, and if your heart interrupts my words with its own, listen.

You are about to love your life - for the first time in a long time, or perhaps for the first time ever. In the next chapter, we're going to begin with something I call the principle of the spark. This concept will make you think about yourself in a whole new way, and it has the potential to make you come alive like never before! But don't skip ahead here. I want you to see how this book can work for you when it's used to the fullest. So start out with the activity and questions below, and let the magic begin!

Do you believe what you just read? Prove it by taking action! Here's what you can do today:

Take out a blank sheet of paper and set it down where you will be reading. At the top, write "As I read this book, I am hoping to _____." Write the first thing that pops into your brain.

Questions to Answer Before You Read On:

I used several nouns to describe you, but you are far more influenced by your own descriptors than by mine. What is your favorite noun to describe yourself? Who do you think you are?

I believe that you are reading this book to invest in yourself. Do you typically enjoy reading? Is it going to be easy or hard for you to read this book?

Have you been changed by the power of words before? Do you expect this book is going to change you? Are you open to change?

"I'm an ordinary man,
Sometimes I wonder who I am;
But I believe in love,
I believe in music,
I believe in magic
and I believe in YOU."

~ Don Williams

Chapter Two

Don't Skip This Chapter ....

because I want to show you how your first crush, best friend, or favorite band can get you more excited about your future than you've ever been!

"We are stardust and miracles - nothing more, nothing less - all of us. And I think that's pretty badass."

~ Steven Floyd

We need to begin here by talking about the spark. Until you understand the principle of the spark, you cannot move forward on this path. So yes, this lesson is the equivalent of the terms and conditions which this screen will force you to open and scroll all the way through before you hit okay. Only this time, you actually need the content. :P

When I speak about the *spark*, I am using language to describe the life force on the inside of a person. Now I realize many are not aware or simply refuse to believe that a life force exists within them. When they are introduced to the concept, they find it ambiguous, vague, and overly mystical - an unhelpful figment of a poet's imagination. So I don't blame you if you are not instantaneously inspired by hearing me say that you have a spark.

Instead of starting with you, let's start with another human being. Let's start with

_____ .

You get to fill in that blank. With what, you ask? I want you to write the name of a person in your life who has made you feel *magical.*

My goal is to be the most magical person you know. I say that all the time, because it's an idea that really does shape my daily life. But you might not have met me, or maybe you aren't familiar with me at all. Still, I know that you have a person who has given you that feeling.

Your first crush. Your first love. The person who walks by at work and gives you butterflies. A soul mate. A best friend. The celebrity you will always pay attention to and pay thousands to meet. The authors whose words have made you weep. The singer whose tracks seem to plagiarize your feelings. You have a person and a name to go in this blank.

If you're reading this on paper, I expect you to physically write their name down. E-book readers and audiobook listeners? You are not off the hook. Don't continue with this chapter until you have identified a name. Use the paper next to you for this name.

Now, close your eyes, take three deep breaths, and just think about this person. What is coming to mind? Why are they special to you? What makes them stand out?

Most importantly, how do you they make you *feel*?

Three deep breaths. Eyes closed. Feel for a moment.

I don't know what just came to mind for you - a roller coaster ride, a walk in the park, the time you told your secret or the day you sat in a movie theater and sobbed. We all just had different memories pop up. What is universal is that we all just felt it.

The spark.

That person you brought to mind has the spark inside of them. You know this reality because you have felt it so many times, and you still feel it. When their name pops up on your phone or a song starts playing or they brush against your arm, you feel the spark, and you know it's real.

It happened to me just this year with a beautiful boy I started hanging out with. Call me a hormonal teenager if you want, but evidently I haven't grown out of this experience. His name, his voice, his face, his laugh - anything was enough to make my heart start beating faster. It's the spark.

This spark is what draws us to people. This spark is what makes people unique and extraordinary. This spark, I believe, is the driving force behind our athletics and our entertainment and our religions and our charity work. All of it moves and shifts and grows because lots of people feel the spark.

It leads us. It draws us in. It moves us. It heals us. It brings us joy. It brings us pain. It breaks our hearts and puts them back together. We know the power of the spark of someone else.

But before you go one page further into this book, I need you to know this:

The spark is inside you, too.

Surely, you knew this is where I was going as a personal life coach, right? Or maybe you forgot all about yourself for a moment because you were lost in the magic of that person whose name is in the blank.

Either way, it's time for you to make the game-changing realization that there is a spark inside of you too.

It's hard for us to believe this truth, because the spark is something that must be felt. And so much is in the way of us properly feeling.

We look in the mirror and see body flaws. We see ourselves as an illustration of the need for Photoshop and the before photo for beauty products and cosmetic surgery. As we stand in the mirror critiquing our human containers, we can't feel the spark. The insecurity of what we see is in the way.

We try to put ourselves out there - at parties and networking events and social media sites. But comparison steals any drive we had before we've even given ourselves a chance. Suddenly, all we can feel is inferiority - our outfits, our resumes, our skill sets, our personalities. Everything looks subpar. Why would anyone else give us a second look when we ourselves run and hide in a hotel room out of embarrassment? As we sit there quietly hoping nobody notices or tries or cares, we can't feel the spark. The insecurity of what makes us different is in the way.

Maybe the real issue here is that we were not created to do life by ourselves. We were not given a sentence of solitary confinement and placed in a world of isolation, but from the moment we entered this human experience, it was clear there was a world waiting to be discovered, creatures which were there for our interaction.

And the spark inside us often has to be spoken to, to be touched by the soul of another. It's as if the spark is only visible through the lens of night vision, a set of goggles which only another human being can hand to us.

People helped to awaken the spark inside of me. When I hated the body in which I moved through the world, a Soul Cycle instructor activated my spark by calling my attention to my strength, my resilience, and my wholeness. When I wasn't sure if I had anything to offer another human being, my friends Micah and Ember gave me whiskey and brownies and helped me realize the spark inside of me was already impacting their lives. When I felt like an outcast in high school because I was so different from all the other guys in my class, my coach taught me to see the spark inside and trust that it would be celebrated someday by the world. Human beings can be the most instrumental in helping us find the spark within.

And that's my job today for you. In this chapter, I'm handing you the goggles. I'm so excited about what you're about to see.

As I write these words, I feel the spark inside me. It's alive. It's beautiful. It's the only one of its kind. I know that it's there, and that it's loving, and that it's good. And my world has stopped for a moment as my spark reaches out across the universe to meet yours.

Do you feel it? Have you noticed it yet? I know that it's there, and I know that it's growing as you read these words.

You have a spark. It is real. It is you. And right now, it is being activated. You cannot ignore the spark any longer.

When you encounter a spark in someone else, you suddenly have to experience it as much as you possibly can. Think back to the person in the blank. Remember what happened when that presence entered your life? You couldn't stop thinking about them, texting them, talking about them. You bought all the albums. You consumed their work endlessly. You made sure everybody in your life understood how perfect they were. You talked about them to the annoyance of all others in your life, because right then, they were everything. Maybe they still are.

But it's your turn now. It's time you become that interested in yourself. I am writing this chapter so that you can develop a curiosity, passion, and intense interest about yourself.

Think about the world that is waiting to be uncovered. Think about the possibilities that have yet to be explored. Think about the feelings and the dreams and the imagination that could fill your life. There's so much waiting for you! And the spark is what makes it worth it.

The biggest mistake people make in life is trying to be someone else. They never find themselves, so they never love themselves. Instead they find somebody else who they like a lot and try to be them. Do you understand why this happens?

If you don't believe there is something within you to be found, you must go "out there" to find it. You have to settle for something external, because you feel like there's nothing to build on inside of you.

I'm here to suggest you do have a starting point - a powerful internal one. That's why the principle of the spark is so important. Your job is much easier than you think it is! You have not been given the task of creating something brand new from the vast world around you. All you are called to do is discover what is inside of you right now, the life you have been given. Once you find that, you can begin creating something external that aligns with and affirms your spark.

Now that you know the spark is there, pay attention. Let it call you. Let it drive you. Let it pull you forward. In the next chapter, you are going to find out where that spark leads you personally as you begin the work of getting to know yourself.

But for now, sit with the awareness of the spark. Trust that it is there and that it will lead you home. As you start to feel that light inside of you, the world is getting just a little brighter.

Do you believe what you just read? Prove it by taking action! Here's what you can do today:

The next time you feel ordinary, boring, or stagnant, put your hand over your heart. Close your eyes and listen to your heartbeat. Recognize that only you have that exact heartbeat. No one else in the world exists to that rhythm. Feel the life force within you. Whether you see a reason to keep trying or not, your heart does. And as long as it is beating, there is something more for you to discover.

Questions to Answer
Before You Read On:
What is it like to feel the spark in the human being whose name you wrote? Write 5 feeling words that describe that experience.

Do you believe the spark in you is just as real and powerful as the spark in _____ ? If yes, how does that realization make you feel? If no, why do you believe you are inferior?

When it comes to _____, what does the spark you feel make you want to do? What action does the spark lead you to? How would your own spark be the same or different?

"I am the spaceman flying high
I am the astronaut in the sky
Don't worry, I'm okay now
I am the light in the dark
I am the match;
I am the spark
Don't worry, I'm okay now"

~ Amy McDonald

Chapter Three

Don't Skip This Chapter ....

because I am about to give you an easy 3-step process for learning about yourself, helping you explore the spark inside of you and providing you with the knowledge of what sets you apart

"Create your own style. Let it be unique for yourself and yet identifiable for others."
~ Anna Wintour

How do first dates make you feel? Nervous? Excited? Anxious? Happy? Indifferent? Most likely, you'd say that it depends on the person.

How about a first date with someone you find sexy and charming? Changes the game right? Suddenly, the date is important. It's an event. It's a lot of pressure, but hopefully it ends up being a memorable experience.

It's time for you to go on a first date with your heart. And you control what you bring to the table here. How much importance will you place on this process? How much of an investment will you make in yourself? Do you believe finding yourself will change every aspect of your life?

Because it will.

Let's get started.

When I meet someone new and am getting to know them, as a life coach or an interviewer or a fellow human, there are three things which I inevitably notice that help me understand them as a unique individual.

I want to share those three things with you, because they will give you unparalleled insight into yourself and the people in your life.

Personality
Question to Ask: What makes me AMAZING?

I begin with personality because this component is the most obvious. Whether it's a consultation for coaching or a first date, a person's personality will always show up in our first conversation. (Frankly, if it doesn't, it's unlikely we will want more conversation.) We relate to each other first and foremost through personality. Personality is the energy you show up in the world with. How you talk. How you move. How you dress. How you dance. All of your likes and dislikes, hobbies and pet peeves, quirks and tendencies.

I know there are endless tests and systems out there to help you find your personality. You can use as many or as few of them as you find helpful. But most of all, know this:

Only you can experience your personality firsthand. It is a destination you must arrive at for yourself.

The question I prompt people to ask about their personality is: "What makes me amazing?"

What do people notice about you when they first meet you? What makes people remember who you are? What do your friends say when they're bragging about you or introducing you to someone else? What makes you stand out from everyone else you know?

These questions can give you clues to your personality. Is that a lot to sort through? Of course! But don't let that discourage you. It's good news that you are a complex and multi-faceted individual.

As you begin to explore this dimension of yourself, you will begin to realize that you are not a boring person. There is so much greatness within you! Whenever that greatness has been lost in the past, it is because you never took the time to explore your personality, or you didn't know you were allowed to express it to the fullest degree.

I refer back to my university experience frequently in this book because it was so life-changing for me. College was particularly important in helping me discover my personality and get comfortable in it. Something odd assisted me along the way in this process.

When I transferred colleges after sophomore year, several individuals at my new college started pronouncing my name "steffin" automatically, which I later found out occurred because of a character on Vampire Diaries. At first, I simply found it strange, as people had never pronounced my name that way before. I had always taken for granted that my name would be read as "stee von." But after a couple times of hearing the new sound, I realized that it felt really natural to me.

Every single word in the universe has a unique vibration to it, and that pronunciation seemed to have a great frequency behind it. (I know how hippie I sound at the moment. Stay with me, and watch what happened.) At the time, I was in the process of discovering the personality which I had long hidden, repressed, and fought. Something affirming happened inside of me when I heard my name pronounced that way.

I suddenly felt like I didn't have to show up in each moment as a product of everything that had happened to me in the past, simply acting out the results of my previous negative experiences. Life felt fresh and new and possible. So I went with it. Though a lot of people got confused along the way, I started using that pronunciation for my name everywhere, because it simply felt correct to me.

You know what's fascinating? The next year, I did research on my family history. I was named after a person of the past, and it turns out my name historically was pronounced "steffin" all along! I made a choice about my identity that felt true for me, only to find out that it was the correct choice all along. (And yes, that's why I have stuck with it.)

The point is - you know when you are showing up as yourself. You know what that feels like. And we need you in our world as that person.

Explore your personality - feel free to change, discard, add, adjust, and tweak anything along the way. Then you can be the person whose spark is felt in every encounter, because your light is shining that brightly. What makes you amazing? Keep searching until you've found it, then never let that go.

Passion
Question to Ask: What makes me come ALIVE?

No matter how stalled life might feel right now, I know that somewhere deep down you possess this element called passion. Maybe your current life doesn't fill you with excitement and wonder, but that says more about your current state than your potential. You have passion inside of you. Everyone does!

I often use one question to help people begin to get in touch with this part of themselves: "What makes me come alive?"

What is it that you do and time flies by? What activity makes you so happy that you automatically forget the stress and sadness of your life? What gives you the feeling of a temporary high without requiring any substances? What makes you smile, laugh, and love more than anything else?

There is something you are passionate about. I don't know what it is, but you do. And you need to know that it is a clue to your destiny.

You do realize that not everybody shares that passion, right? Even if they acquired all the information you have, processed the same experiences, and met the same people, everybody wouldn't experience the same feeling you do there. That's precisely why passion is a crucial clue to this increasingly less nebulous idea of yourself.

Only you get <u>that</u> excited about <u>that</u> thing in <u>that</u> way. Your passion is unique to you. Other people may share interests or hobbies or skills, but the spectacular way that you come alive when a specific intersection of people, situations, and experiences come together only happens for you.

You need that information. I know for many of you this process hurts, because for so long you were told to ignore your passion.

I relate to your frustration here, because as a child, I loved to dance. I had an innate sense of rhythm, even as a small kid, and I couldn't keep my feet from moving to each and every beat. My body instinctively felt the music, no matter what music happened to be playing at the time. I loved dancing. I was passionate about it.

But I ignored those glimpses of my heart. I mentally minimized them and emotionally numbed them. My parents told me dancing was evil. My friends told me it was for girls. My relatives told me it didn't result in a stable career. So I didn't pay attention to my passion.

Left dormant, your passion will begin to fade. Mine did. But the amazing reality is that passion never completely goes away. Nearly a decade later, my passion was awakened again when I accidentally signed up to be part of the feature musical at my university. I got to dance, on stage, to a jubilant score with a beautiful cast of people who meant the world to me. And I felt my passion awaken inside of me again.

I'm still pursuing this personal passion. In fact, I just completed my first modern dance class as I wrote this book. And I'm on this journey right now because I believe our passions were not meant to be ignored.

As you begin to get in touch with this part of you, you'll find that you have lots and lots of passions.

Some of your passions will reveal to you the work you are meant to do full time. My passion for speaking, connecting the dots in my life, and empowering other people led me to become a personal life coach. But some of your passions are just there because you're alive. I would suggest they're actually there to help you come alive. Dancing for me was not about making money or making a name for myself. It was about the experience of moving my body on that floor and on that stage, an experience that I know made me more of myself.

What makes you come alive? Keep looking until you've found it, and then put that in your life for as long as you live.

Pain
Question to Ask: What makes me ANGRY?

"Noooooooooo," I hear you groaning. "This book has been so positive and upbeat so far. Why did I just read the word pain? Why are you making me think of stuff that triggers anger? Why?!"

That's one response that some people reading this book just had. Other readers are in the middle of so much pain right now, they're relieved to hear me acknowledge life isn't just one big self-help conference.

Either way, I think it's vital that people ask themselves, "What makes me angry?"

You can't skip this step. You can't get around the question.

Maybe when you hear the word 'pain,' you first think of sadness, hurt, and grief. It might come as a surprise to you that I would use a term like anger.

But I'm talking about deep pain here. Not the kind that makes you sigh and drink a glass of wine. The kind of pain that prevents sleep, makes you shout and scream at the sky even though you feel no one's listening, and creates a restlessness inside of you that demands action.

That pain is a clue to your true self. And it may hurt like hell to sit with it, but there is only one path that ends up at a destination containing a self that has been found. If you choose this path, you cannot skip pain. It's that annoying fountain that sprays you on the lazy river. You can hate it all you want, but the tube only goes one way once you've hopped in.

Your pain is important... That was supposed to be the start of a sentence at first, but then I thought it needed to stop there.

Your pain is important.

I wanted to write just those four words and leave them there first, since so many of you feel the exact opposite. Maybe your pain has been downplayed, ignored, denied, dismissed, and if it has, I am so, so sorry.

The people that told you your pain was a sin were wrong. Your pain is exactly what you need to feel right now.

The people that told you your pain was weakness, they were wrong. Letting yourself own that stuff is the strongest and bravest choice you could ever make.

The people that told you your pain didn't matter were wrong. It does matter. Your hurt is felt by the universe. Your sorrow is connected to universal grief. Your pain is essential to who you are, and you must feel it to be human.

Your pain is unique. Everybody knows what it's like to feel pain, but you're feeling something unique in a way only you can.

And your pain gives you clues to what you are called to do.

That issue that makes you angry? There's something you are here to do about it. That problem in the world that keeps making you cry? You are here in this moment to meet that challenge with a solution. That person that has broken your heart and wounded you so deeply you don't think you'll ever recover? Even there, a lesson is waiting for you. In all of the pain, you are going to learn. You are going to heal. You are going to take action. Your pain is all being used to point somewhere.

But you must give yourself permission to have that pain.

What makes you angry? Keep looking until you find it, and then do the work to figure out where that pain is pointing.

All of these questions are intensely personal. It's okay if you feel a little apprehensive diving in to answer them. Just know that you deserve to know the answers for yourself. What do you do if the answers bother you? Hang in there. In the next chapter, I'm going to walk you through how you can process everything that's happening inside of you as you learn and grow.

For now, let me just say that all of these questions should ideally be asked of you continually. It's not an exercise that you can do one time and be good forever. These questions can be answered for the rest of your life, and they should be! What makes me amazing? What makes me come alive? What makes me angry? At the intersection of those questions is the soul that you are - your SELF. At the core of all of your answers, you will find that your true SELF - that thing you used to think movies made up, that voice you didn't know you had, that person you had no clue where to find - it has been there all along. It has guided you and embraced you and supported you, just waiting for the day when you decided it was worth finding.

Breaking News: Today is that day.

You found it.

Look yourself in the mirror and say hello.
Because things will never be the same.
Do you believe what you just read? Prove it by taking action! Here's what you can do today:
Before you go to sleep at night, write down one statement that reminds you just how unique you are. Start out with "Only I ..." and go from there. The possibilities are endless. What do you bring to the table that no one else can? Think back through your day and write something to finish that

sentence. Do this for a week, or better yet, a month, and your confidence levels will skyrocket.

Questions to Answer

Before You Read On:

What parts of your personality do you love? What parts of your personality do you dislike? What percentage of your personality do you feel you are comfortable revealing to people in your life?

Is there anything you would feel embarrassed or guilty for being passionate about? What is something you are passionate about that you've never admitted to anyone?

What is your default response when pain pops up inside of you? Do you feel as though you know how to handle pain, or do you run from it?

"Don't be scared,
there's someone there to say
these words you need to hear.
You will never find yourself anywhere else.
You'll find yourself in you."

~ Amber Hezlep

Chapter Four

Don't Skip This Chapter ....

because after you read it, you will never view your emotions the same way again! (Hint: they're about to become your best friend.)

"The best and most beautiful things in the world cannot be seen or even touched.

They must be felt with the heart."

~ Helen Keller

I hope you're enjoying asking yourself those key questions more and more. What makes me amazing? What makes me alive? What makes me angry? Those questions are always an easy way to find yourself.

Of course, I'm assuming here that you actually did thoughtfully answer these questions. :) (See why you needed the blank paper nearby?) If you haven't yet put your answers on paper, take a moment to write them down. That's a part of this book that only you can contribute. The book will be lacking if you don't participate here.

Once you've done that work, the answers will begin to reveal to you exactly who you are, I promise.

Who you are is unique. Who you are is special. Who you are is perfect. I know you are standing in your truth more and more each moment.

But as you get to know yourself, it's quite likely you will run into feelings - perhaps feelings you haven't been in touch with for a very long time. And that can be terrifying.

I remember a point in my life when I did everything in my power to avoid feelings. I wish that was an exaggeration, but that accurately describes the mindset I had at the time.

I purposefully booked my schedule so full that there was no margin time that might allow me to pause and feel something accidentally. I filled every spare moment with media of all kinds to borrow the feelings of other people, which were far easier to handle than my own. I came up with defense mechanisms for myself, so if I ever came too close to feeling too deeply, especially in public, I knew how to exit the scene and change my emotional state immediately. No joke - it's hard to believe for those who know me now, but I had prevented myself from feeling at all costs.

And then life got hard. Hard as fuck actually. Somebody broke my heart. One of my best friends' partners left him. A friend of mine was sexually assaulted, and I was diagnosed with a mental disorder as an adult. All within a month. I repeat, life got hard.

The hardest part of dealing with all of that was that I attempted to move forward without feeling. I thought I could find a way out on my own without the help of those annoying things called emotions. Boy, was I wrong.

Despite the external business, distance, and distraction that I maintained, I wasn't able to prevent feelings from popping up inside of me. After all, no amount of calendar invites could take away my humanity. Feelings showed up, alright. And after I ran from them for as long as I could, I finally had to confront them in therapy.

Now, I've been to therapy four times. I think all of us need it at some point in our lives. Ideally, we won't need it forever. Counseling is designed to help us deal with the past, revisiting our memories and learning how to heal and recover. Life coaching, on the other hand, is much more present-minded, focusing on the life we are currently living and the future we want to create. With that distinction in mind, it's probably evident why therapy is often much heavier and more burdensome for people. The past can be a shitty place to return.

But sometimes, we all need it - even life coaches, ministers, authors, and teachers. Especially life coaches, ministers, experts, and teachers.

The biggest gift of therapy for me that particular time was learning the skill of getting to my feelings.

When I started seeing a counselor in the midst of all of that pain, I admitted from the start that I didn't remember how to feel - that I felt like I had lost track of all of the feelings within me. I knew walking into my first appointment that I hadn't even opened the lid of the massive crockpot that my feelings had become.

I only knew how to think. Years of high school debate and a large dose of cable news had taught me how to form intellectual arguments and articulate them. I could talk about my thoughts endlessly.

But I didn't know how to get to my feelings. I blocked them without even meaning to.

I knew I had been avoiding feelings to an excessive degree that month. I didn't feel ready to start dealing with any of my pain yet, and I knew it. But my therapist showed me that I had actually been unable to deal with my feelings for a long time. This revelation dawned on me when she asked the following question:

"How did you feel when your dad kicked you out of the house?"

"Well, I guess I felt like he just got to choose not to be a parent."

That was genuinely what popped into my head. I wasn't lying to my therapist there. But that was not a feeling. That was a thought, an opinion, a personal perspective.

I knew that I felt something about the situation, because it was a turning point in my life. Yes, I got kicked out of the house as a teenager. Was a person to blame for that? Yes. Was a system to blame for that? Yes. But despite all the time I had spent thinking about what happened and talking about it, I hadn't let myself process it through feelings.

After I sat with my therapist's question for a little while, I finally arrived at this answer.

"I felt abandoned. I felt betrayed. I felt shocked. I felt furious. I felt hurt."

See the difference there?

Healing happens when we finally get to the level of our feelings.

So yes, I'm telling you to embrace them.

Your feelings are what make you human. Although other creatures in our universe experience physical sensations and have nervous systems, science has proven that no organism has the ability to feel as deeply as the homo sapien. I think that fact makes our feelings a gift - something precious, something special, something rare and important and valuable.

The more we run and hide from our feelings, the less human we become and the further we get from our true selves.

There is no way to get to your true self without involving your feelings.

Don't guilt trip yourself for experiencing feelings. Instead, be thankful that you are human and alive and a recipient of the beautiful gift of a heart. You have every right to feel everything you need to feel. In fact, more than that, you have a sacred obligation to honor the life you have been given by letting yourself feel whatever it is your human experience is causing you to feel.

How do you start doing this if you've trained yourself to do the exact opposite?

Here's the exercise that saved my life that difficult painful month:
> When I think about _____
> I feel _____
If you want to go deeper, add this:
I feel _____(from above)
which makes me afraid that

_____.

That exercise is so powerful! Not only will it move you from thoughts to feelings, it also helps reveal the fear that is often lurking just beneath the surface, making our feelings seem so insidious and awful.

One of my favorite mentors, Iyanla Vanzant, helped me understand that my feelings are energy.

Everything is energy. This foundational principle of science and spirituality helps me make sense of the world. From the stuff that appears to be 100% solid matter to the stuff we know is real but can't see at all, it's all energy. That is the truest way to understand our universe.

That means our feelings, just like every other component of reality, are nothing more and nothing less than energy.

Why is this so crucial to comprehend? Because energy is always in motion. It is not static. It cannot be at a standstill. Also, it's never destroyed. It never just disappears. Energy will always and forever be in motion.

If you reflect for a minute, you'll know intuitively that this is the case.

I'm sure you can remember a moment when you could tell a feeling was headed in your direction. Grief, loneliness, heartbreak, anxiety, anger, jealousy - it's often the negative ones we see from afar, isn't it? But you know what I'm talking about. You can recall the sense of a feeling getting closer and closer, maybe too close.

We often feel threatened by this. We sense a feeling is about to hit us, and we devise a plan of evacuation as if we desperately need to escape a deadly storm.

The problem is, no matter what plan we devise, the feeling will not disappear. That point is essential, and yet, that point is not understood by 99% of individuals.

Feelings don't just disappear.

If you do indeed, find a way to bypass a feeling, you merely chose a strategy of manipulation. You found a way to manipulate the energy. But please be clear - the feeling did not disappear.

You may have *projected* it onto someone else. You may have *repressed* it in your subconscious. You may have *buried* it deep within your memory. But it didn't disappear. The energy is still there.

And if you do that long enough, your heart will get sick. You will literally feel the tension created by all that manipulation.

All those feelings you thought you were rid of will come back to haunt you. They will show up through interactions with random people in your life, dreams you don't care to acknowledge, thoughts that keep you up at night, pain that randomly hits you for no reason. Who knows what will trigger these feelings? But you will feel them eventually. Because they are still there.

So what should we do? When we suddenly perceive that a feeling is headed towards us, how should we react?

Here's a better question: What would happen if we embraced that moment? That feeling? That experience?

Instead of trying to repel it or dodge it or minimize it, what if we just said yes?

I believe if we can say yes to those feelings, they won't last forever.

They're energy remember? Always in motion. They don't naturally get stuck.

So when a feeling hits, keep breathing. Let air flow through your body. Let your heart beat as it always faithfully does. And let the feeling pass through you.

Maybe it will be momentary, or maybe it will spend the night. But it will not last forever.

If you can be with it, sit with it, even if "it" brings a lot of discomfort, that feeling will keep moving. It will move through you, and you will move on. You will move forward.

You will be free to move because you let the feelings move in you.

I have found one of the most helpful exercises for me when I am stressed or anxious or emotional is to just get out a piece of notebook paper and start writing down how I feel. You still have your blank sheet with you? Try this exercise.

How do you feel right now? How did you feel when you woke up this morning? How do you feel thinking about the future? Start writing down the words that come to mind. Write each feeling down in a full statement. I feel _____.

Somehow, that seems to help me and my clients. When our feelings are down on paper, they're less threatening. They aren't quite as terrifying. We can see them for what they really are, an experience which we are having that is only an experience - not the defining word on our life forever.

I think a lot of people are scared to embrace the experience of a feeling because they are scared it will lead them to a dark place. I understand that nervousness.

But feelings do not dictate your beliefs. You can experience absolutely any feeling and then choose absolutely any belief.

Give yourself permission to feel. Then, give yourself the investment of carefully choosing beliefs.

You can love yourself - all of yourself, including those feelings you think will make it impossible. We'll begin that work in the next chapter. Right now, all you need to focus on is accepting the feelings that are showing up. You can't love yourself until you know what's happening inside of you.

If you are science oriented, you may find it interesting that research tells us an automatic emotional response in our bodies typically only lasts 90 seconds. Do you find that as fascinating as I do? 90 seconds. A minute and a half. It sounds so manageable, doesn't it?

There are feelings which seem to last much longer, even when we don't want them to. So maybe that fact isn't always helpful. But I think there is at least a little encouragement in the brevity of that. 90 seconds makes it seem like feelings aren't the scariest thing in the world anymore.

I hope this chapter gives you permission to be human. If you've been seeking to find yourself on an intellectual level, while simultaneously resisting anything happening in your heart, I hope you realize now that your heart is the only place you will ever find yourself.

When you are feeling the most, you are the most alive. And in that place, as what you feel reveals your personality, your passion, and your pain, you will finally find yourself.

Do you believe what you just read? Prove it by taking action! Here's what you can do today:

The next time you experience a strong feeling of any kind, pull out your cell phone and open a new message to send to yourself. Type "Because you are loved, you have permission to feel _____." Use the most descriptive, vivid word for what you are feeling. And then let yourself receive that message, open it, and believe it. Even if you don't feel completely convinced your feelings are okay, keep tangibly giving yourself permission. Do that enough times, and soon your feelings won't seem like such a threat.

Questions to Answer
Before You Read On:
Do you personally spend more time thinking or feeling? How quickly are you able to get to your feelings?

What feeling are you most afraid of? What is your defense mechanism to avoid feeling this?

Do you have any feelings that last much longer than 90 seconds? Which ones? Why do you think they last so long?

"My body moves
Goes where it will
But though I try
my heart stays still
It never moves
Just won't be led"

~ Chris Martin

Chapter Five

Don't Skip This Chapter ....
because I want to help you understand why your current attempts to raise your self-esteem aren't working and what you can do to really change the way you feel about yourself

"You have the approval of yourself. That's quite enough for we who know true inner peace."
~ Charmaine Smith Ladd

By the time you've reached this point in the book, you are finally beginning to see a clear picture of who you are. You have been asking yourself the types of questions that reveal your personality, your passion, and your pain. As you continue to notice your feelings more regularly, you are becoming more in tune with the unique individual that you are.

But unfortunately, you may have realized discovering your true self does not automatically result in loving yourself. If you have ever studied theories of identity development, you know that the journey of learning who we are as individuals and then accepting ourselves is a long and messy process. Countless theories in the world of academia try to suggest how the average person can do just that.

Although these theories differ in many respects, after you've read enough of them, you start to notice trends. One major trend I've observed is that in nearly every model of identity development, following the point of self-discovery, there is a required shift from tolerance to acceptance.

Think about and feel those two words. What does the word *tolerance* feel like to you? What does the word *acceptance* feel like to you? Do you notice the difference?

Tolerance is the essential starting point for compassion. That's why it is so emphasized in our society right now. In a world full of discrimination, prejudice, and marginalization, people need to be taught to tolerate people who are different. Tolerance, at the political, social, and cultural level, will prevent us from choosing speech or actions that harms other people groups, which is a definite win.

However, tolerance is not an ideal end goal for us to hold personally. When you reach the point of self-awareness (the goal of Chapters 1-3 by the way), you initially may find yourself at this place of tolerance. In this stage, you are able to see yourself as a unique human being. You recognize that in so many ways you are different from the people around you. But you may not be entirely sure how to feel about this reality. Is your uniqueness actually an asset?

Your personality comes with quirks that other people don't have. Are those going to embarrass you? Will you have a harder time living with a partner or working with a team because of them? Many people end up insecure precisely because they have recognized how unique their personality is.

Or ... you're passionate about things nobody else is passionate about. Does that mean you're crazy? Should you tone it down? Why doesn't everybody else love that too?

Or ... you feel pain when everybody else is complacent. That means you might end up at odds with people you care about. Should you speak out? Should you fight that urge and remain silent? How can you get to a place of peace?

As you sort through these questions, you will find yourself either getting stuck in tolerance or moving towards acceptance.

Tolerance = I know who I am, and I don't like it, but I guess I have to find a way to live with it.

Acceptance = I know who I am, and I love being me!

You can reach a place of acceptance. It is indeed possible for you. But there is one essential truth you must understand about acceptance.

Only you can bring yourself into a place of acceptance.

This truth is crucial. So many people recognize that they only tolerate themselves, or worse, can't stand themselves, and they try to move to acceptance vicariously through another person.

That never works. That never works. That never works.

Let's say you're insecure about your body. You hate the way you look. You can't stand having to stare at yourself in the mirror every morning. You get stressed just buying clothes because it's a reminder that you've gained weight. You drive a different way to work every day so you don't have to pass the gym and feel guilty. At this point, even using the word *tolerance* to describe your feelings about your self is a stretch.

Now, the worst thing you could possibly do in this situation is think, "Gee, if I had a boyfriend/girlfriend/significant other who was into me despite my body, I wouldn't have to deal with all of this insecurity."

But many people get to that point and do exactly what I just described. They think that the only way they can get to a place of acceptance is through the approval of someone else.

So they start seeking it. They look for acceptance at work, at school, at religious communities, at nightclubs, at networking events, etc. The list goes on and on.

It keeps going indefinitely because their search for acceptance goes on indefinitely. The secret which is being kept from them is that none of those people, environments, or activities can give them what they are looking for.

Live that way long enough, and you will literally find yourself addicted to the acceptance of people. You will constantly need verbal affirmation. You will depend on always receiving a steady stream of invitations to events you don't even want to attend. You will feel as though you need a significant other in your life at all times. I'm not exaggerating - this need for external acceptance will literally become an addiction.

And that turns every one of your relationships - personal, professional, and romantic - into a codependent one. You are not in the relationship with a full heart able to give love away. You are in the relationship because you NEED it. You don't know how you'd survive, much less thrive, without it. You are using every person to fill a void in your heart that you simply refuse to fill yourself. This is a mess.

Self-acceptance must be an internal process.

It's difficult to do the work, I know. It goes against how many of us were raised. It often takes a fight - deliberate choices to trust our inner voice, to honor the life we've received, to stand in our truth, and to celebrate our humanity. But whether you're doing great at the moment or whether you're struggling with acceptance, your life is worth the fight.

As a gay man who grew up in fundamentalism, I found it so incredibly difficult to accept myself. I had been trained to hate myself - the way I dressed, walked, talked, acted; the media I liked; the people I was attracted to, the dreams I held for my life. I had learned how to reject all of that. The best I did for years was a public tolerance and a private self-loathing.

But one day I made the choice to believe a different story about myself. My favorite author Rob Bell says that the Gospel is the hope that you can believe a new story about who you are, that a new word is being spoken over your life, that you can trust this different and better narrative.

How do you change the narrative and start loving yourself? I think it all starts with our beliefs.

A **belief** is nothing more than a repeated thought which you have chosen to embrace and implement in your life. If you are unable to love yourself, it's probably because you have embraced and implemented some really harmful beliefs - that you are unloved, ugly, unwanted, not worthy, not good enough, etc. (In the next chapter, we'll look at the number one source of our harmful beliefs.)

If these have become deep roots within your soul, it will take work to get them out. But your beliefs aren't permanently stuck. When you decide to repeat new thoughts into your life, embracing them and implementing them, slowly by surely your core beliefs about yourself will change, and you will arrive at self-acceptance.

Here's how I began that process:

I took an hour and wrote out everything that I knew to be true about me. Statements from sacred texts. Statements from my favorite books. Statements from film quotes, song lyrics, tumblr graphics, Oprah episodes. Most importantly, I filled this document with statements that came from within - who I knew I was called to be, what I knew was true for my life.

It wasn't just enough to write them. I had to memorize them, to soak them into my heart, to plant them in every area of my life. So I began to read the document out loud. The first week, I read it every hour. Literally. If I wasn't in a meeting or a session or sleeping at the time, I would find a place to go read it out loud. And this was not a 45 second reading. It took a good five minutes. But I knew I needed it.

I kept reading it, over and over and over. And when I started, most of those words did not feel true. I did not feel beautiful. I did not see a life of abundance in front of me. I did not always sense that I was making a difference in the world. But I kept reading.

Eventually, I limited it to five times a day, then two times a day. And when I finally survived a winter physically and internally, I felt comfortable just reading it at the beginning of each day. And you know what? I'm still reading it. I'm still updating it. Those words are now so lodged in the core of my being that they flow through me with every heartbeat, every intention, and every word spoken.

Now, I don't try to remember them or implement them. They guide me. They heal me. They remind me.

That embedding doesn't happen instantaneously. If it did, it wouldn't be so meaningful or permanent. But it works over time. Just like the splendid air freshener I have plugged in to the wall in this room right now, the new elements you desire to fill your life with take time to get there. But be patient and don't give up. One day you'll look around and realize the sweet aroma of self-acceptance has arrived.

That's the secret. That's what I know to tell you in this chapter. I can't make you believe you're worthy, and there's no product you can buy to accomplish that either. But you can start saying it - every day, with your hand over your heart. You can hear your own voice say that you are loved. You can feel the power behind your own breath declaring that you are magnificent. You can sense the energy moving through you as you declare that you have purpose.

Then one day, I really believe, you will say those words for the hundredth time. And it will suddenly dawn on you. You don't feel as though you're reading a script anymore. You aren't talking yourself into anything. Now, you are just telling the truth. And you have been telling the truth all along.

Do you believe what you just read? Prove it by taking action! Here's what you can do today:

Start every morning by looking at yourself in the mirror. Smile at yourself. NEVER look at your body with a look of disgust or disapproval. Say out loud, "I love the honor of getting to be me, and I completely accept the body that I exist and move within." Then hug yourself - a rich long hug that you stay in for a few seconds. I don't know how this works, but it changes you from the inside out. Anyone who's tried it can back that up.

Questions to Ask
Before You Read On:
Do you feel like the word tolerance or the word acceptance more accurately describes the way you feel about yourself right now?

Where do you tend to look for acceptance externally?

What are your deepest beliefs about yourself right now? Are you open to the idea of changing those beliefs?

"Wait a second.
Why should you care
What they think of you?
When you're in your room
By yourself
Do YOU like you?"

~ Colbie Caillat

Chapter Six

Don't Skip This Chapter ....

because I show you how shame might be ruining every area of your life and give you a realistic plan for ending that cycle once and for all

"Shame, blame, disrespect, betrayal, and the withholding of affection damage the roots from which love grows. Love can only survive these injuries if they are acknowledged, healed, and rare."

~ Brene Brown

One of the most important authors and speakers of our time, Brene Brown, has identified shame as a deadly toxin that eats away at the root of love in our lives. She is famous for exposing the destruction and havoc that shame causes to our personal relationships, and I have felt its effects there firsthand.

But I believe shame is also toxic to our ability to love ourselves. When I began to try to find a way to love myself, I constantly found myself fighting a battle against shame, and I didn't know what to do to beat it. Many of you are there right now. Yes, hello. I'm with you in this struggle.

There are a lot of academic and technical definitions of the word *shame*, but I don't think they are the most helpful in identifying and calling out this menace. I personally prefer the way Carl Jung described it: "Shame is a soul eating emotion."

Shame is a negative feeling about *who you are.* That's the easiest way to understand it. Shame differs from guilt in this way.

Guilt is a negative feeling, just like shame, which is why it's often confused with shame. People sometimes think they are identical feelings, just under different headings in a thesaurus. But there is an important distinction. Guilt is a negative feeling about *what you did.* Shame is a negative feeling about *who you are.* See the difference?

Let me give you two examples from my childhood. When I was a little kid, I cheated only one time in school. Ever. I didn't believe cheating was right. I never justified it in my mind. The one time I did it, I couldn't think straight or eat the rest of the day. My internal moral compass told me stealing another person's work could not be justified. But I cheated once on a math paper.

That entire day, I felt <u>guilt</u>, more strongly than I had ever experienced before. (Clearly it left an impression, since I still vividly remember that day.) Guilt said I needed to feel badly because I had taken credit for someone else's work. Guilt told me I was going to feel bad until I owned up to what I had done. Guilt warned me I would never be at peace making a choice like that.

And that day, I let that guilt guide me to talk to my teacher about what happened. I wrote her a letter and said sorry. I redid the assignment or had my grade lowered, something like that. Honestly, I don't remember, because all that mattered to me at the time was that I got to make it right. Guilt was at work in that situation. And it wasn't necessarily a bad thing. Guilt helped me make a better choice in the future and make restitution using negative feelings about *what I did.*

But here's another example from my childhood. I guarantee you that you're even going to feel different while reading it.

Around the same age as I was in the first story, my parents did ministry work all summer on the West Coast. From teaching at religious schools to holding church services to sponsoring special events, we traveled on the west coast doing the work of God (meaning, I traveled with them and read books while they did this work). Now, on one of these trips, I went to Disneyland for the first time. That was the day I decided my life was always and forever going to be magical. When I rode Dumbo for the first time, and walked through that castle for the first time, I felt more wonder and joy and delight than I had ever felt before. Disney helped me find the spark inside of me, it really did.

So naturally, I was still talking about my first experience at Disneyland the next day, the next week, the next year really. And it ended up getting me in trouble.

Evidently, (though I had no recollection of this conversation at the time), an adult at church had asked me about my summer. They were hoping to hear about my parents' spiritual work, expecting great stories about all the people whose lives had been touched. Instead, they heard a 10 minute monologue about how spectacular Disneyland had been.

When I got in the car later that night, my dad chewed me out about it. He told me it was embarrassing and humiliating for him that I had done that. I was clearly too irresponsible to be representing our family. What was I thinking? I probably needed to be grounded from Disney if it was that problematic for me.

What I remember so distinctly about that night was feeling the emotion of *shame* for the very first time.

I sat in the car and cried in silence. See, a very different dynamic was at work here. I didn't feel bad about what I had done. I barely remembered the conversation, and I didn't feel as though I had done anything wrong. But I was shamed.

I felt like a disappointment. I believed I had let my family down. Clearly, I was a screw-up. I couldn't do anything right. It seemed I hurt people without even trying. I didn't know better, but obviously, that proved I was stupid. I was so blind to what I was saying …. These were the kinds of thoughts going through my mind. And that was my first experience with shame. Huge difference.

Guilt = feelings about what you did
Shame = feelings about who you are

Now, there is correctly placed guilt and misplaced guilt. If someone accuses you of something you didn't do, that guilt will not serve you in any way. If a person guilt trips you for not making a choice you had no intention or desire to make, that guilt should be ignored. I'm not saying we just receive any and all guilt. But I am saying that guilt <u>can</u> be there for a reason. It <u>can</u> be there to point us to create lives of integrity, something we'll explore in the next chapter.

Shame, on the other hand, serves zero purpose in our personal growth. Guilt *may* be a spiritual teacher for you. Shame is never a spiritual teacher. It is not your friend. It is not your guide. It is your enemy, and the enemy of your self-acceptance.

If you feel shame popping up in your life, it's time to do work. What does shame look like? What does it feel like? What does it sound like?

Shame is ...
You are a failure
Nobody wants you. Nobody likes you
You aren't good enough
You are ugly
You are never going to get better

(Let's make this practical. Fill in yours.)

Shame is bad enough when it comes from a voice inside of us. It's even worse when it comes from people we care about. The sad truth is, many people try to use shame as a way of controlling behavior. Parents realize that if they shame their children for certain decisions, their kids will behave differently. Bosses realize they can use shame to get their employees to cooperate. Manipulative friends realize that they can shame people into conformity, and manipulative significant others realize they can utilize shame to get what they want in a relationship if the person is vulnerable enough.

Shame works on a lot of people. That's why it's so often the go-to choice of behavior and leadership. But it doesn't have to work on you. Not anymore. Those voices, whether internal or external, don't have to get through to you any longer.

The good news is, shame has a kryptonite. Shame cannot survive under the power of love. Love defeats shame, every time.

Love says that no matter what you did which may have caused guilt, you are loved. You are lovable. You are love itself. That is the truth. And because of that, you have nothing to be ashamed of.

Here's the best way I've found to fight shame:

Only believe thoughts about yourself which are true.

Remember all the work we did in the last chapter going through our beliefs? It's time to use that skill you have again. That is how you will begin to fight back against shame.

Do not simply be a sponge for every thought that pops into your mind. Not all thoughts can be trusted. And do not automatically accept every thought which a person speaks into your life. Not every person knows who you really are. Only believe thoughts about yourself which are true.

If the thought you are processing is loving, you can believe it. If the thought you are considering comes with the premise that you are loved, it's trustworthy. If the thought in question reminds you that there is love already inside you, it's a keeper. Loving thoughts are true because love is the deepest reality.

But all of that shame? All of the beliefs that come with it and result from it? They are not love, and they are not true. So don't accept them.

I know, it's much easier said than done. But you have to start somewhere. And if scientists are right that your brain goes through 80,000 thoughts every day, there's plenty of material there to begin working with. Your beliefs can be replaced much faster than you might initially predict.

Start today. Start this hour. Start with the next thought about yourself that pops into your mind. Is it true? Is it true about YOU? Does it come from a place of love?

You get to choose what you believe, and you don't have to settle for shame.

Nietzsche said it beautifully: "What do you regard as most humane? To spare someone shame."

Spare yourself first. Then spare others. Then you'll understand why sacred texts promise that as long as you get the love part right, everything else works out just fine.

Do you believe what you just read? Prove it by taking action! Here's what you can do today:

Next time you realize you have allowed a false and harmful belief to enter your mental space, remove its power through forgiveness. If you're alone or with trusted friends, you can speak out loud. Otherwise, speak mentally to yourself, and say, "I forgive myself for believing _____." The minute you do that, you don't have to deal with guilt for wrong beliefs, and you have the freedom to make any other choice.

Questions to Ask
Before You Read On:
Can you recall a time when guilt helped you? Can you recall a time when guilt hurt you?
Do you think people in your life use shame to try to control your behavior? Do you find yourself doing this to others?
What is one negative belief about yourself that you can discard and forgive yourself for today? What loving thought can you replace it with?

"Show me how to walk with you upon the waves
Breathe into my spirit
Breathe into my veins
Until only love remains."

~ JJ Heller

Chapter Seven

Don't Skip This Chapter ....
because it will open your eyes to the limits on your life that you don't even realize are there and show you how the principle of integrity is crucial for every decision

"Be who you are and say what you feel, because those who mind don't matter and those who matter don't mind."
~ Bernard M. Baruch

It's time to be yourself! I finished this section last when I wrote this book, and I was so excited to finally get here! I admit, this topic sounds like it belongs in a Disney Channel sitcom or in the middle of tween pop lyrics. But it's one of my favorite topics to discuss, mainly because I know this subject is tricky for so many people.

We've heard about it and sung about it and thought about it. But we still don't know how to be ourselves, or what that even means! And I'm not talking about middle schoolers here. I'm talking about the countless adults with successful careers, picture-perfect families, and large social networks who come to me for help because they still haven't gotten this right yet.

Being yourself is not as simple as you might at first assume. It's a paradox, because in many ways it's the easiest assignment of your life, and simultaneously, it might be the hardest to live out.

Being yourself is an assignment only you can complete, a call only you can answer. It's going to require individuality.

Note. Individuality is different than isolation. Isolation is trying to do everything on your own, living life by yourself. Isolation happens when you choose not to be involved in any communities, making sure you keep a safe distance from people in your life. I'm not recommending isolation. Science, psychology, and religion all suggest long term isolation is dangerous and unhealthy.

Also note: Individuality is different than independence. Independence often involves a person thinking they must do everything by themselves, refusing to collaborate and avoiding asking for help. This mentality can show up in an entrepreneur who refuses to hire an assistant, a partner who won't admit they are struggling, or an employee who still dreads working with a group just as much as they did in college. Independence sounds good on paper and boosts our ego, but it's actually not the most efficient or effective way to get things done. Experts in communication, productivity, and task management all confirm that you need other people to work alongside you for the best results.

So what am I talking about then? I'm telling you to be an individual - to be the human being that only you can be. The 90s punk movement many of us lived through was on to something by telling us not to conform. While of course I do recommend driving on the correct side of the road and following the understood courtesy norms of a social network, there are many places where conformity is dangerous. Conformity can be fatal to your dreams, your ideas, your passion, and your destiny.

Right now, at this point in your life, you are living by a set of rules. Don't write me off immediately here. Think about it for a second.

I'm not saying you're necessarily religious or somebody who's never broken a law. But as you make decisions and more importantly define a vision for your life, you do play by a set of rules. We all do.

The question becomes, whose rules are you living by? Where did you get those rules from? Do you even realize how many rules you have accepted as parameters for your existence?

What kinds of rules am I referring to? All the knowledge you have accepted and implemented into your life about:

What people are like
How the world works
What is possible for the future
How you should treat your dreams
What your career will be like
What to expect in relationships
What skill sets are worth your time and investment
What people will pay for
What people value
What people like and accept and love

Now, I'm not telling you to throw out all your marketing books and go yell at your teachers. A lot of this information has been helpful. Much of it was probably 100% true and accurate. And it may have gotten you to where you are today.

This kind of information only becomes a problem when we unnecessarily turn what we have heard into a **limit**. Up until a certain point, the information we have been given guides us and directs us and moves us forward. Then we reach a point where it suddenly feels different.

We find ourselves wanting to try something or create something or do something that doesn't fit into the model that's worked for us so far. What do we do in those moments? More specifically, what do YOU do?

If you give up, try to forget the idea, and keep maintaining the status quo, you have allowed yourself to live under somebody else's rules. That idea that was inside of you? It just might have been possible. It could have been the next big thing. Who knows if it wasn't a tiny seed with giant potential to change your life, or the entire world?

Use the information you've been given as an individual, but NEVER let what you've heard or read or experienced in the past prevent you from answering the call on your life.

You are responsible for your life. That includes the voice inside you and everything it calls you to do. Don't ignore that voice to follow rules that don't fit. When a jacket doesn't fit anymore, it's time to donate it. Same principle applies for rules which no longer serve you.

You don't have to curse the rules or condemn them. In fact, there might be someone else who would benefit from them at the exact moment you no longer need them.

Just step into all that you can be and all that you can do. Play by the rules that come from within - that's individuality at its core. And it results in a life of **INTEGRITY**.

People often have a very limited conception of integrity. I asked a client the other day what he thought integrity meant, and his first thought was taking an oath not to lie in a courtroom.

STEPHEN LOVEGROVE

Certainly, I would hope a person of integrity would be truthful in a courtroom, but integrity is so much more than that.

To me, integrity is a life where your beliefs and intentions are aligned with your words and actions. It's that basic and fundamental. And yes, it's that challenging and hard.

Integrity is so much more than simply choosing not to tell lies. It means you are always acting authentically, at every given moment, in every possible way.

Integrity begins with your beliefs. It starts when you take ownership of your beliefs - rejecting beliefs that harm yourself or others, and carefully selecting beliefs that are true and healthy and beneficial.

When you can do that, integrity moves to your intentions. You do realize that every single choice you ever make is motivated by an intention right? Conscious or unconscious, it doesn't matter, because your intentions are just as powerful either way.

If you don't understand the power of your intentions, read a spiritual teacher like Gary Zukav or Abraham who can explain in great detail how much creative power you truly have. But know this: your intentions affect everything that follows them. Every. Single. Time.

If you smile at the person in the cubicle next to yours, but deep down are hoping they got sick and

78

disappeared for a few days, the true intention in your heart will eventually be felt in that environment.

If you apply for a new job but inwardly don't believe you deserve it and are making other plans, your intention will come across even while you interview.

If you put yourself out there on an online dating website but are secretly terrified that you are not ready for a relationship, your unconscious intention will sabotage your success there. It just will.

The sooner you can take ownership of your intentions, the better. And this is vital to your integrity. It's not enough to just say and do things that others approve of. All of our lives must flow out of loving intentions.

And yes, it will be evident and obvious in our words and actions.

When we live with integrity, we will say what we mean as clearly and kindly as possible.

When we live with integrity, we will do only what we are called to do, doing it with excellence, care, and passion. We will not do things we secretly want to get out of. We will not do things without knowing the WHY. Our words and our actions will start to have an exponential effect, because they are in alignment.

That's when the magic really begins. When your beliefs, intentions, words, and actions are all on the same page, life is spectacular. You celebrate all of the experiences flowing into your life, because you know you will enter them all from an authentic place.

In my own journey, integrity was neither easy n or automatic. It was such an extensive process, to be honest.

I had to consciously let go of beliefs which I hadn't actually taken seriously for years. I had to take responsibility for my unspoken intentions which were leaking into my outcomes. My journey into integrity required me to stop saying words that sounded nice but weren't real for me. Most of all, it necessitated that I take action, over and over. The universe ensured that I learned this lesson by giving me choice after choice after choice to make that tested my willingness to be authentic.

The summer after my sophomore year of college, I knew I needed to come out of the closet publicly. Yes, all of my family and friends already knew. It wasn't like I was going to shock the people closest to me with an unexpected announcement. But I felt a deep calling to tell my story. I believed sharing my experience could help somebody else who was feeling alone. I knew it was the right moment to talk about my sexual orientation online.

So I did. And my employer wasn't happy with it. They informed me in a meeting that by coming out to the internet, I had become a public relations issue for them. And that week, I lost my job and my financial aid and a number of friends. Ended up having to transfer schools and start all over again.

You know what astounded me the most during all of that, though? It wasn't the part that angered the nation and made headlines. It was what happened on the inside of me. See, I walked out of that meeting, fully knowing my life had just changed drastically. But I wasn't angry. I wasn't scared. I wasn't even tempted to reconsider my decision to be honest.

I proudly left the room and said a prayer of gratitude, because I was so thankful for the opportunity to choose integrity. From the minute I posted my story online to my decision in that office to stand in my truth, I had acted out of integrity. And that was all I needed to know.

Integrity helped me love my life more than just about anything else.

If you start to work towards integrity - one day/choice/intention at a time, you will feel the shift. Every area of life will be noticeably different, as people experience you showing up in a different way. But it will be a change for the better, I promise. You can only get to the life that was meant for you by being the person you were always meant to be.

Beliefs, intentions, words, actions - all in alignment with the unique individual you are. When individuality operates out of integrity, you, my friend, are unstoppable.

Do you believe what you just read? Prove it by taking action! Here's what you can do today:

The next time you find yourself struggling with a decision, pull out a piece of paper and start listing categories. Create headings for (A) Beliefs, (B) Intentions, (C) Words and (D) Actions. Then go through and list what is happening inside of you. I have found that the minute we see this on paper, we instantly understand why there is so much tension within us. And when we have all four aspects laid out so clearly, we can circle which one is right for us, and use that as our guiding light to integrity.

Questions to Ask
Before You Read On:
What gets in the way of you showing up in the world as an individual? Do you tend to struggle with independence or isolation? Or are you confident showing up as yourself in groups?

Which piece of integrity is hardest for you to keep in alignment - beliefs, intentions, words, or actions?

Have you ever acted out of integrity and been grateful for it? Have you ever acted without integrity and regretted it?

"Call me selfish if you will
my life I alone can live
I say I got to be true to myself."

~ Ziggy Marley

Chapter Eight

Don't Skip This Chapter ....
because it's my absolute favorite in the entire
book and the only one that will ensure you receive
everything that was meant for you in this year of
your life

"The present moment is filled with joy and
happiness. If you are attentive, you will see it."
~ Thích Nhất Hạnh

So we have experienced the shift of self-
awareness, begun to work on our self-acceptance,
and started to embrace our self-identity in the work
of integrity. Before we go any further, I want to
honor that.

I am so proud of you for taking the time to not
only read this far but also to have done all that work
to invest in your personal growth. Very few people
take a book like this to the next level by actually
doing the work and implementing the value.

But before you try to do any more work or add
anything else to your life, you have reached my
favorite chapter of the book. It's the chapter that
most clearly helps you translate time spent reading

this book into a magical everyday experience. Why did I wait so long to get here? Because it wouldn't have worked without a foundation. You had to find out who you were first. There's no getting around that if you intend to love your life. And you had to figure out how to accept that person. I hope you feel so worthy and so loved today, by the way. You are ;)

You even needed a discussion on integrity first, because it is out of that place that anything positive will come.

But with all of that transformation behind us, we need to talk about the single greatest gift you will ever receive as a human being.

the present moment

Every single one of us has this gift. We will always have this gift as long as we are human. It is what makes us alive. It is the purpose for the breath inside our lungs. It is the calling which is always speaking to our hearts. Yet many of us have never even been told this gift exists.

I remember learning about this gift for the first time when I was attempting to restart my life after getting fired for my sexual orientation. As you can imagine, that was a particularly difficult season of my life, and I was looking for answers.

What I thought I needed and what I actually needed were two very different things, however. Isn't that often the case for you, too?

The week I got fired, I remember meeting with a mentor of mine. We had previously written all of the various activities which were a part of my life on a marker board in his office, allowing me to have a visual aid as I tried to plan out my time management. Although I hadn't intended to create a dramatic effect with that board, it ended up being quite a memorable moment. Because that day, I came into his office to an empty marker board.

Of course, it was empty because my previous session was a distant memory at that point, and numerous people had used and erased the board since then. But I couldn't help but apply the visual to my own life.

The board had been filled with all of these roles, positions, activities, and functions. And in one week, because of one decision, they had all ended. I had to relocate and start over.

And I will never forget my mentor asking, "Who are you without anything on the marker board? What do you have now?"

I didn't have an answer for him that day. I was speechless. But you know what I discovered? After sitting and thinking and being open in that space for a couple months, I realized I had something extremely valuable, even with an empty marker board. I realized that in the midst of my frantic sea of duties which I had visualized in EXPO ink, I had missed the most precious thing I had all along.

the present moment

You have it right now. You are in it right now. How's it going?

I was guided to a book called The Power of Now by Eckhart Tolle, a book that wasn't afraid to ask, "What problems do you really have in this moment?"

The book helped me realize I had been living my life all wrong. In any given moment, I was attempting to live in either the past or the future.

I would find myself trying to live in the past through regret - wishing I could go back and relive a happy memory; mourning the loss of something which had left my life; imagining how I would do something differently if I got a retake.

OR

I would find myself trying to live in the future through fear - worrying about my finances; stressing about my career; trying to play out in my brain every possible scenario that could happen at a later date.

In either case, I didn't know how to live in the present. I wasn't even trying. It was as if the present moment showed up as a beautifully wrapped gift with a glittery bow on top, and I looked to the right or to the left and complained that I saw nothing.

The problem with living in the past or the future is that it makes you think you are broken right now. It convinces you of the lie that this moment, the current one, is incomplete.

And the reality is, this moment contains everything you need. This moment is the right one for you. This moment perfectly delivers to you the lesson your soul is ready for. (And what you do with this moment determines what future moments show up. More on that magic next chapter!)

So the only way to be yourself is to be present.

I know it's easy to think, "If I could only work with that designer, or if I had a record contract, or if that person would notice that I exist, I would be so much happier! It would be so much easier to be myself if I could afford that outfit, if I got to work there every day, or if I was able to live in that city!"

On and on the distractions go, pulling us out of this moment into one that is not real. We sit in the past and grieve, for we think we have left ourselves behind there.

We look to the future and tremble, for we think that our true self is out there somewhere fading into the distance away from our reach.

And yet, our true self remains in the stillness - just beneath the surface - waiting to greet us in the present moment.

What does it mean to be YOU? How do YOU like to show up in the world? Those answers have to be lived into. But I promise you this. They are not hidden. They are not elusive. They are not locked away in an attic of your past, and they are not under the hood of a shiny car in your future. What it means to be you is a truth you can learn right now In this moment. And later today, in that moment. And tomorrow morning when you first wake up, in that moment. (Need I go on?)

Who you are is unique. There is an essence to who you are that is boundless and magnificent. There is intuitive guidance on the inside of you that is wiser than you could imagine. There is spirit on the inside of you that will make your heart soar and could even inspire the world.

But only by you being present will you access that.

Only by you being present will we get to experience that.

I don't know if you like Jesus or hate Jesus or are just apathetic, but I want to reference a teaching of Jesus here that helps this reality sink in.

Jesus once taught a group of people that they missed him. Which was a strange comment for him to make, given the fact that these people were quite a fan club. They followed him everywhere and refused to leave him alone. We're not talking LA photographers here - this was Australian paparazzi level.

But Jesus tells these people that they missed him. His own fandom missed him.

"HOW?!?!?!?!?!?!?!?!" I imagine they would have posted on tumblr if it had existed at the time. "HOW DID WE MISS YOU?!?!?! JFC" (Get it? It's ironic because ... okay moving on.)

Jesus tells the audience that they missed him because he showed up in the form of a person that simply needed a drink of water. He showed up in the form of a person who couldn't afford clothing for themselves or their kids. He showed up in the form of a homeless person who needed food. And they missed that.

They turned away from that moment, and in doing so, Jesus said they missed Jesus.

See, Jesus had already communicated the idea that there was divinity on the inside of every person. He taught people the powerful affirmation that "the kingdom of God is within you." When people challenged the new age sounding claims he made, Jesus quoted an ancient sacred text which calls every human being "gods of the most high." Jesus really believed there was divinity in all of us.

So for Jesus, every interaction was an interaction with the divine. Jesus didn't just want people to obsess over him and trample others and stand in line for hours to hear his talks. He wanted them to honor God by honoring the sacredness of all people and all life.

Every single moment is a chance for us to interact with the divine. As Brandan Robertson says, all of life is prayer because all of life is an opportunity for us to commune with our higher power.

That's why being present matters so much. That's why every single moment is such a valuable gift.

Because whether we are at Cafe Gratitude or Carl's Jr, whether we are in a cathedral or in a nightclub, whether we are inside of a mosque or on the metro, every single moment is a sacred moment. A moment far too important for us to miss.

When we miss the people and the experiences and the feelings of our lives, we miss God. We don't get to know the joy of seeing God show up in the world. More profoundly, we don't get to participate in the wonder of God showing up in the world.

If there is anything I know for sure, it is that being present is what God wants us to do. Being present is what we are here to do. Being present is the best way to honor the life you have been given, and the only way to truly be yourself.

Don't miss another moment. Don't miss God. Don't miss this chance to be yourself - you can only do that in *this* moment.

Ready? Go .....

Do you believe what you just read? Prove it by taking action! Here's what you can do today:

The next time you feel hopelessly distracted and unable to be present, get still and mentally use this question.

"What gift am I about to miss in this moment?" You'll be far less likely to let yourself miss something beautiful after centering yourself in that way.

Questions to Ask
Before You Read On:
Who do you believe you are in this moment? Do you have a sense of identity separate from your past history and your future plans?

Do you find yourself trying to live in the past or the future more often?

What is the hardest environment for you to believe could be the source of a divine moment? How would you act differently if you believed that could result in a God moment?

"The future is right now
right in front of you
Don't let the clock tell you what to do
Our future is right now
I'm right in front of you
Baby, don't blink and miss
this moment"

~ Katy Perry

Chapter Nine

Don't Skip This Chapter ....

because I am going to explain why I see the world as a magical place and try to prevent you from making the most common mistake people make when trying to change their lives

"The day I understood everything was the day I stopped trying to figure everything out.

The day I knew peace was the day I let everything go."

~ C. Joybell C.

Welcome to this moment. :) I don't know when you are reading this chapter, but I do know that you now understand how important this moment is, how perfectly everything must have come together for you to get here right now. So welcome.

As we learn to embrace the present moment together, understanding that being ourselves means being present, it's important for us to now talk about control.

Control is a tricky thing in the world of self-help books. There's a lot of different opinions and contradicting advice out there when it comes to this fascinating question of control in your life.

Now as a Sagittarius, I find the deep questions of philosophy and metaphysics fascinating. My mind is intrigued by concepts like string theory and fate and individual free will. Most likely, that's not your personal go-to bar conversation.

But I do think it's important to figure out how much control we individually have within our own lives.

There are self-help books out there that will tell you that you have zero control. Control is an illusion, they'll say. You actually have no control over what happens in your life. The art of living is learning how to just accept absolutely anything.

Problems: Does that mean my shitty dating relationship is the universe's fault? My lack of going to the gym is just the fate I was given?

There's also self-help books that will tell you that you have complete control. You are literally in control of every single thing that happens. Don't ever think somebody else caused something to happen in your life. It's all you, they'll insist over and over.

Problems: Who in their right mind would blame an assault on the victim? And a person born into poverty should've fixed it themselves before they got to college? Really?

Turns out control is a little more complicated than many would have us believe. I think the best spiritual gurus of our time are the ones that can acknowledge that tension. I question anybody who claims to be an expert but is unwilling to do so.

Here's what I believe. We have control over ourselves at every single moment. We don't control the world. We don't control other people (or at least, we shouldn't.) But we are in control of our experience at all times.

I love the way my mentor Oprah Winfrey puts it: "You have complete control over your own energy field." YES! That's the truth.

Let me illustrate this.

If I go to a party, I can't control what types of people show up to attend. I can't control if they flirt with me, ask me out, or even find me attractive. That can feel frustrating, because it means even deciding to attend is taking a risk.

BUT I can control whether or not I go to the party. I can control what my body language conveys. I can control what conversations I initiate and which I avoid. And I can control whether or not I leave my heart open. See how this works?

If you mistakenly think being yourself means trying to obsessively control all of the people and events in your life, you'll get frustrated. You just can't do it.

So please, for the love of God, stop texting that person who clearly doesn't want to talk. Have the courage to admit that person you like just isn't into you, and move on. Give up your endless quest to get that coworker on your side who just has a completely different personality. Being yourself does not mean dictating everyone else's experience for them.

On the other hand, if you mistakenly believe being yourself means complete apathy, wake up! Don't stay in every weekend and then complain your life is boring. Don't sit on your phone in the corner and cry about having no friends. You do have power in your own life - and a lot of it! You do get a say in your own experience. Being yourself means you step up and choose how your life plays out.

Our power lies in our own energy field. That's the bottom line. Most of us have barely tapped into it there, and have endlessly tried to use it elsewhere. We would be amazed at the results we would see if we would give up our useless pursuit of control in other energy fields and maximize the power in our own.

You are an energy field, after all. In the most literal scientific way, you are energy - particles in motion within a force field, just like everything else in this universe (review from chapter four).

And you are constantly radiating out some type of energy. Whether positive or negative, strong or weak, that energy can be measured and felt and witnessed.

It is vital that you claim your power in your own energy field and choose what you do with it carefully, because whatever you choose to radiate will come back to you. The ancient law of karma, just like the principle of reaping what you sow, confirms on a spiritual level what science tells us happens on an energetic level.

The energy you send out into the world is attracting more of that energy into your life. So, as you take complete control of your energy, it will feel like you have control in all kinds of environments in the world, simply because how you show up impacts everyone and everything around you.

Trust that when you decide to be yourself, the universe will most certainly rise up to meet you every time. It can rearrange itself infinitely to align with the energy you are bringing.

What will happen when you claim your power? What could happen when you start showing up? What might be possible when your energy changes completely?

The best thing you can do is show up as your unique self, bringing your personality, passion, and pain to this moment.

That's terrifying, right? Because you don't know how people will respond, and as I've been saying over and over throughout the chapter, you can't control how they feel about you. I know how much of a chance being yourself and releasing control can be from firsthand experience, and in the next chapter, I'm sharing three extremely personal stories that illustrate what can happen when we make that choice.

But research indicates simply taking responsibility for yourself and showing up at your best in each moment does, in fact, bring the best people into our lives. Researchers for an online dating website found that when people carefully crafted a generic profile that they thought would appeal to the masses, they had the least success. In an attempt to control their experience on the site, they had actually driven away most people there, especially the people that would have been a good match. Because their goal was to make sure nobody would say anything bad to them or about them, they ended up coming across as unremarkable, literally.

If you try to appear normal to everyone, attempting to control how people respond to you in every situation, you are only hurting yourself. In the end, people will think you're normal, but that will translate to them missing your greatness. They will view you as average and fail to see the unique soul that you are. Even if you succeed at convincing everyone you are normal, you have failed at what really matters. Because you have ensured nobody will see you as extraordinary.

I'd much rather be extraordinary. Wouldn't you?

I'll close this chapter with my all-time favorite Rumi quote: "Live life as though everything is rigged in your favor." That's not so far from the truth you've discovered recently, is it?

You are a powerful being. You are an energetic being. You are showing up as yourself, and the entire universe is at this moment rearranging itself to meet you there. That sounds pretty damn good to me. Maybe the odds are in your favor after all.

Do you believe what you just read? Prove it by taking action! Here's what you can do today:

Find a place you sit/stand in front of regularly and post a quote that brings you back to a positive outlook of claiming your power. The Rumi quote works wonders for me! "Live life as though everything was rigged in your favor." Imagine the subtle shift that will occur in your mind when that quote greets you day after day. You'll feel the difference!

Questions to Ask
Before You Read On:
Do you feel like you have control over your life?
What area of your life right now feels the most out
of control?

Do you believe that you have a say in your own
experience? How much do you think the way you
show up affects other people?

Do you believe the odds are rigged in your favor?
How much do you trust the way the universe is
working right now?

"Stand up, speak up, dream big
For you are the dreamer.
Try harder, whole-hearted
Reach higher!
The sky is the limit
Claim your power."

~ Marcela Pinilla

Chapter Ten

Don't Skip This Chapter ....

because I'm talking all about my first kiss, my first date, and my first love! It's vulnerability at a whole new level from me, ending with my love letter to you.

"The privilege of a lifetime is being who you are."
~ Joseph Campbell

I don't know about you, but for me, this journey has been wonderful. I hope you feel the same way. Figuring out who you are, learning how to love that person, and starting to show up as that person in your daily life are choices you never regret. I am so glad you have stayed with me til the end.

I wanted to leave you with 3 stories from my own life, showing you how these principles work in my own life - both when I ignore them and when I follow them. And the stories I felt called to share in this chapter were my first kiss, my first date, and my first love. Get ready.

My first kiss:

I had just come out of the closet to people. At this point, I wasn't comfortable with the idea of being in a relationship, definitely not with the thought of getting married one day. Truth be told, though I had come out, I wasn't even entirely sure how I felt about being gay at this point.

But there was a boy in my class. He was kind and funny and smart. He had cute blue eyes and a decent body, and he was the first guy who had openly expressed attraction to me in person.

I found myself in his dorm room on his couch. He invited me over to do homework one night. And I know this story reads like one from Boy Meets World (or Girl Meets World, which I also enjoy), but I was indeed having this experience as a college student.

We were cuddling, and I knew things were going well. But you need to understand I had no clue how to act in this situation. I had never even held a boy's hand at this point!

So when he leaned in to kiss me, I tried to kiss back as soon as I figured out what was happening. It was a mess.

So much of a mess that he asked me, "What? Do you not like kissing or something?"

(Told you this book was the most vulnerable I've ever been. That's an embarrassing moment right there.)

Now, as I look back on this moment, I see positive and negative. On the plus side, I didn't have a traumatizing experience. So many people have their idea of intimacy tarnished by a horrific experience they can't forget. I am thankful I never went through that. I can't imagine how horrific that must be.

Also on the plus side, it was moving forward for me to finally acknowledge my feelings. This came at a period in my life where I was finally okay with having a stereotypical gay personality in many ways. I finally owned the fact that I liked boys, including this one specific boy, and that I wanted to get close to him. All of that was actually good for me.

But that moment was fairly meaningless. We hung out once more, and then it never went anywhere. You're not shocked?!

Seriously though, while it wasn't a tragic memory, nothing about that moment felt authentic for me. It didn't come from an internal place. It didn't make me feel anything on the inside. It was just an event that happened, showing me I did need to own up to my feelings but also showing me that I set the bar for what I wanted to show up in my life.

My first date:

Sadly, I didn't learn the lesson right away. Funny thing about life: When we don't pay attention to what is happening in our lives, we miss the lesson that we were meant to learn. And when we miss that lesson, the universe works perfectly, and it shows up all over again.

So a month later, I find myself on my first date ever. No, I did not count playing video games with the boy from school and my #messymakeoutmistake a date.

This was a blind date with someone online who had a couple cute pictures. At the time, I thought it was going to be magical. I was so excited when I got dressed and got in the car that night! Annoyingly enough as I reflect back on it, I drove nearly an hour to meet this guy at a movie theater for the midnight premiere of a movie.

The date went okay. We didn't kiss. He was definitely a cuddler, though. At least I got free popcorn. Never saw him again. And that is about the extent of the feelings I had about that date.

At first, I couldn't figure it out. I was so enthusiastic and positive beforehand! Why had the entire thing turned out to be mediocre?

Well, when I started to examine it more closely, I realized that once again I had acted in an inauthentic manner.

I didn't take the time to get to know this boy. I barely knew anything about him. This first date should have come with zero attachment, since I really was meeting a stranger. Instead, I tried to pretend I already knew we were compatible.

I actually ignored warning signs - interests, beliefs, quirks, factual realities which I had knowledge of from his profile that could have warned me he wasn't a good fit. Problem is, I didn't set a high bar at that point. I didn't set a bar of any kind. I just wanted a date. I was willing to run any amount of red lights to force an experience I thought I needed right then. Bad idea, kids.

And the worst part is, I didn't even want to see the movie. It was a superhero sequel, and I won't tell you which hero because I don't want to alienate an entire fandom. But I did not have any desire to see this movie, and I didn't end up enjoying it. I put myself through all that gas money, all those drawn out action scenes, and all that awkward conversation just so I could say I had been on a date.

Needless to say, this was not remembered as a positive experience. The lid on top of the kale juice (this book is too healthy for ice cream/cherry metaphors) was finding out six months later this guy had developed a reputation for going after sugar daddies. If you're unfamiliar with that term, don't worry about it. Just know my selection of men here was pretty awful.

In both of these stories, what was the common denominator? I settled for a surface understanding of what I wanted. I did not take the time to find out what I was really looking for. I did not love myself enough to let my needs, desires, and feelings set the bar in my life. And I was willing to give up being myself to force experiences to happen. Finally - finally - finally - I learned this wasn't the way. Which brings me to my third and final story.

My first love:

I had known this boy for so long. From the beginning, he was just a friend. That had always been clear in my mind. Even when he became a close friend, a best friend, a trusted friend, he was a friend. That was clear.

Until one day it wasn't. And one day I suddenly started tumbling down the spiral staircase of doom that is falling for a friend.

I had always thought he was physically attractive, and that wasn't a secret to him or to anyone. But now I had feelings. Not erotic ones. EMOTIONAL ONES. The worst kind when it comes to friends you are not supposed to feel like that about, right? Maybe you've been there, and if not, may gratitude flood your life in this moment.

So this friend came to visit me one summer and we spent an entire week together. Though a good portion of our friendship took place long distance, we were now hanging out in person. It was magical. I loved every second of it.

But halfway through the week, I also knew I was totally fucked. When I found myself crying in bed because of the sheer emotion of the week, I knew these feelings were at a whole new level. Never before I had cried about a boy - any boy - much less one with so much history.

So in dramatic fashion, on the very last night of the vacation, I said three words. I took the biggest risk of my life. It felt like it then and it still feels like it was now.

I'm a public speaker, and usually I have no problem saying things, even really difficult things. But I literally tried to start speaking and nothing came out. My mouth moved, but it wouldn't make sound. And then words came out, but the wrong ones. And then I sat in silence for 20 minutes and told him I needed to collect myself.

Finally, I said it.

"I think ... that .... I love you."

I said it, and it was even more terrifying than I had feared. And after I said it, there was silence followed by,
"Uhh, I need to think."

OBVIOUSLY THAT WAS THE WRONG RESPONSE. HADN'T HE SEEN GOSSIP GIRL AND LEARNED ANYTHING FROM DAN HUMPHREY?

That is literally what happened - no exaggeration or embellishment. To try to reduce the awkwardness even by 1%, I turned on the Kardashians and stared at the screen.

It didn't help.

I still get sad thinking about that moment. It would be nice if the story ended differently - if he had burst into tears and professed his love for me; if he had said the same three words back and hugged me; if he had given it thought and then asked if we could try a relationship.

But you know what? I said those three words to a boy who didn't love me back, at least not in that way. He casually dropped a "love you" later on, and in a platonic 'you have impacted my life' way, he was telling the truth. But I knew. He had given it thought, and we were not on the same page. I built up all this courage to say "I love you" for the very first time, and I said those words to a person that couldn't reciprocate them.

But guess what?

I don't regret any of it.

That friendship. That trust. That openness in my heart that let feelings get in. That summer. That week. That choice to make the best memories possible while we had the chance. That night. That silence. That decision to say those words that could have ruined absolutely everything.

I don't regret it.

My first kiss I regret. My first date I regret. But I do not regret the choice to say I love you for the first time. Even though that was the melodramatic story. Even though that one ended badly. I don't regret it.

Because that time, story #3, that night, I was myself. I found my feelings and honored them. I loved myself enough to trust what I felt and say what I needed to say. And I chose to be myself. I was present as I delivered my awkward speech and felt each pound of my beating heart. I had never been more of myself than in that moment.

Why did I tell you that story? And why would I end this book with that story? These are valid questions because I almost left it out entirely.

I chose to put that story in here because I needed you to be clear about something. I can't promise you that if you find yourself, love yourself, and be yourself, you will never get hurt. I am not promising you a life free of pain, and I certainly cannot guarantee that the road ahead of you will be comfortable or easy or conventional.

I got my heart broken, dammit. I did everything I was supposed to do on an internal level, and I got my heart broken.

And yet, after a million plays of the Coldplay album and healing conversations and endless meditation and journaling, I finally got it. None of that was wasted. The feelings. The risk. The heartbreak. None of it was a waste. None of it had to go to waste if I refused to let it.

At every point in that process, I was being healed. Even at the most painful moments of that story, healing was available. My soul was learning and growing and changing. My heart was opening and glowing and expanding. All of it was worth it.

While you might think the choices that leave no regrets behind are the minimal ones and the casual ones and the safe ones, I believe the opposite is true. Regret happens when we are still left with "what if." Regret is the result of leaving a story within you still untold, a song inside of you never sung, a touch unique to your personhood that never was felt by another. When you lay everything on the line because you believe that much that the life you have been given is the utmost calling to be answered, you don't regret it.

So I wanted to leave you with a love letter from me to you:

Remember that spark?
From back at the beginning, the one you didn't even know you had?
It's still there.
Aren't you grateful it came to wake you up?

You did the right thing doing all of that work to find yourself.

You did the right thing taking all of that time to learn how to love yourself.

You did the right thing deciding to do whatever it takes to be yourself.

I am so fucking proud of you.

As I am writing this, I feel a weight from you, reading this whenever you do.

I feel the weight of people that left, friendships that collapsed, dreams that failed, injustice that prevailed, shame that wouldn't leave, pain that didn't hurt any less when you thought it would. I feel all of that.

But none of that is enough to hold you down.

I promise.

None of that is reason enough to keep your heart shut. I know you will find a way to keep it open.

None of that is dark enough to extinguish the radiance of your light. I am confident you are still shining.

None of that is ugly enough to even slightly tarnish the love that is you. I feel the love from you as I write, knowing this book will reach you in perfect timing.

Keep opening your heart. Keep shining. Keep loving.

From a boy who found a magical soul, a heart worth loving, and a person worth becoming in the same body that once looked in the mirror with no hope,

I promise you can love your life.

Love,

Stephen

Do you believe what you just read? Prove it by taking action! Here's what you can do today:

The next time you're about to take a risk that scares you to death, pause and use this question to determine if you should proceed:

"Is this coming from me, or is this coming from fear?" The right decisions are ones where you have to push past fear to honor yourself. The wrong decisions are ones that involve giving in to fear even when it means betraying yourself.

Questions to Ask
As You Finish Reading:
What is one decision you made in the past that did not feel authentic to you? What was the outcome?

What is one decision you made to be true to yourself that was extremely difficult to make?

Is there any decision you know you need to make now in order to be yourself, but you are terrified to make?

Love After Love
by Derek Walcott

The time will come
when, with elation
you will greet yourself arriving
at your own door, in your own mirror
and each will smile at the other's welcome,

and say, sit here. Eat.
You will love again the stranger who was yourself.
Give wine. Give bread. Give back your heart
to itself, to the stranger who has loved you

all your life, whom you ignored
for another, who knows you by heart.
Take down the love letters from the bookshelf,

the photographs, the desperate notes,
peel your own image from the mirror.
Sit. Feast on your life.

Conclusion

I'm speechless. My breath is gone. I won't employ any more clichés here, but as I finish the task of writing this book, which I knew I was called to do, I am so humbled.

Writing this book changed me in so many ways, many of which I never expected. That's how I can confidently say I know it has changed you too. To the degree that you entered this conscious space with an open mind and heart, I know you have been transformed just as I have along this journey.

As I say goodbye for now, at least in this setting, I want to leave you with one more thought:

You are a change agent.

The universe changes when you change, because we are all connected. That's why Gandhi tapped into infinite wisdom when he said, "Be the change you wish to see in the world." It's true on so many levels because when you change, you are an active presence and force of change in the world. The world is different because you are different.

Of course, you've learned so much that you may automatically feel compelled to share it with people. That's not a bad thing! Just remember, not everybody will be immediately eager to start processing feelings, choosing beliefs, being present,